the Gift of Flowers

A personal story
and practical guide
to flower arranging
by
Beverley Parkin

WM. B. EERDMANS
PUBLISHING CO.
255 JEFFERSON AVE. S.E., GRAND RAPIDS, MICH. 49502

Thank you to Peter, Jeremy, Guy and Charlotte — also to the friends who lent their homes as settings for the photographs.

Photographs by David Alexander
Illustrations by Rachel Beckingham

Library of Congress Cataloging in Publication Data

Parkin, Beverley.
    The gift of flowers.

    1. Flower arrangement. 2. Parkin, Beverley. I. Title.
SB449.P29   1976   745.92'092'4   75-38549
ISBN 0-8028-3479-5

$4.95

Contents

The point of it all   7

Principles of
flower arrangement   14

Arrangements in the home   20

Classic shapes   27

Miniatures   32

Dried flowers and   35
collages

Colour   42

Flowers in towns   47

Special occasions   51

The gift of flowers   58

Index to botanical names   61

The point of it all

Women are creative creatures, as a rule. We give birth, make homes and cook (to varying degrees of perfection!). But this is not always enough. We sense somewhere deep in our personalities the need to express ourselves, but do not know quite where to begin.

This book is for those who are looking for some means of doing so. It is also for those who have little time or ability or money to spend on what they may feel is a rather secondary occupation: flower arranging.

As a wife and mother of three growing children I sympathize with those who lack time and money. But I believe that I have been given the ability to create beauty in my home – given, as I now believe, by God. So I would like to share what I myself have been taught. Step by step we will tackle what I hope will become a new hobby for many.

I also hope that, for some at least, it may prove to be rather more than a hobby. This has certainly happened in my own case. And as I have mentioned 'expressing personality', it may interest others to know how this came about.

How it all began

I grew up in the city rather than the country, but was fortunate to be able to stay for some of the time with my grandparents on the coast. Some of my earliest recollections are of my grandfather taking me on what seemed interminably long walks to my short legs. We went to see the young lambs. We foraged for early primroses in the woods. Then followed cowslip-picking and later we gathered large, luscious blackberries. I remember not only the baskets overflowing with fruit but also my hands being slapped, as I preferred eating the fruit from the basket to scratching myself on the brambles!

On leaving school I had an interest in fashion, and was fortunate to secure a position in the showroom and as a behind-the-scenes-girl at a top fashion house. I was sixteen and very naive, and the long hours came as rather a shock. I think the only mark I left there was my unpunctuality.

I was a typical teenager – unpunctual, impatient, obstinate. My world revolved around me.

Then all that came to an end. I contracted polio. I was in hospital for about six months and received much care and attention. But it was a shattering blow. Although I apparently looked quite happy and cheerful, underneath lurked the question, 'Why me?'

I racked my brains for an answer. What terrible sin had I committed that merited such a punishment? These feelings gradually subsided, and I returned home to my parents with many muscles very weak and total paralysis of the left arm, which proved permanent. My parents made me exercise hard and as I gradually grew stronger I worked in my father's office – and I met my future husband.

The 'therapy' of flowers

It was also then that plans were made to send me to the Constance Spry School of Floristry. This was made possible by a dear 'adoptive uncle' who always held the opinion that nature was therapeutic. In the years that have followed I, like many others, can affirm the truth of this.

In the past few years I have taught flower arranging for an adult education school. Some of the people who come seem to look on flowers as their own personal enemies. They handle them like instruments of war! This is only because they lack confidence in their ability and have not really opened their eyes to the beauty and perfection of the creation they are handling. As their confidence increases their shoulders relax, the strain lines around the mouth lessen and their eyes become brighter.

This is not fanciful – I have seen it happen many times. The Eastern cultures discovered it hundreds of years ago. Eyes are gradually awakened to the beauty of living things. The introverted personality begins to look outward and life can be full of new interest. Perhaps we can even look at one another in a new light.

All kinds of possibilities

Many live in cities where green spaces are fenced off. Picking even a leaf or twig is frowned upon. Trees – where there are any – are dusty and polluted by traffic fumes. The eye aches for a glimpse of fresh green leaves and the colour of a flower. Hearts cry out at the lack of these things. It is very natural to say, 'How can we experiment? We haven't gardens or hedgerows from which to gather – so we don't stand a chance.'

Wild flower pedestal

This beautiful arrangement was made entirely from wild flowers picked near my home.

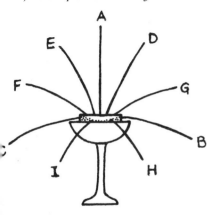

The shape is technically called a free fall pedestal.
The flowers are lady's bedstraw, scabious, foxglove, ragwort, cow parsley, sorrel, knapweed, white campion and grasses.
Oasis is used on a gripholder – protruding 1 inch/2½ cms above the vase.
A B and C are the same lengths. A is inserted two-thirds of the way to the back of the container.
B and C flow downwards from the pedestal.
D E F G are graduated in length towards B and C.

H and I curve downwards from the front.
Fill in the outline with graduated lengths of flowers. Cut some stems fairly short, so that there is interest throughout the whole arrangement. Place the most striking flower or foliage low centre front for your focal point.
This is a very graceful design and may be used for any size of container, from a wineglass to a large church arrangement, the main stipulation being that one must use plenty of curved foliage or flowers for the outline.

Don't despair – start looking! Most cities have markets where flowers are cheap. Wait until the season is well under way and flowers are being sent up from the country in their boxfuls. Many of the trees that line the city streets are pruned during the year, and twigs die off naturally and fall to the ground. Bare twigs can be very beautiful – watch out for them. An expedition to any waste ground will secure some interesting stones and very often that treasure of all wild flowers, rosebay willowherb – which can turn the ugliest disused sites into pink glory. You may also find grasses, daisies and some of the ragwort family.

There may also be possibilities for window-boxes or tubs, and we will discuss this in a later chapter. If you are able to go away on holiday there are rich opportunities. Perhaps you know someone living in the country. If so, don't be afraid to ask them for fresh flowers – most people are delighted to share their produce.

As we become aware of the glorious treasures that are around us, as we open our eyes, it is natural to question how and why. This is how I myself was brought on a further stage in my discovery.

Taking independence too far

I was married in 1957. I had been encouraged back into independence by my parents, and I carried this on into my marriage. This was a relief to my husband, who had thought (he said later) that he would have to do a great deal more than his share in the house. Despite my weak muscles and having the use of only my right arm, we coped and I managed to work and run our little home, my husband loving and encouraging me throughout this time. Our three lovely children were born and by then we were fortunate enough to have our own house and garden. Although there are many gadgets on the market designed for disabled housewives I refused to have any, on the grounds that they would clutter up my nice, newly-decorated kitchen. One can carry independence too far! We had some help in the house, for which I was most grateful, but I justified this on the grounds of having three small children rather than because of my disability.

My flower work continued to some extent. I really regarded it as a means of escaping from the day-to-day routine. We moved house again and then there followed crisis after crisis. I broke my left arm, injured my back and damaged my eyes – not all at the same time, I hasten to add. But as a result I found myself dependent

With Jeremy, Guy and Charlotte in the kitchen at home. In the centre of the table is a small vase of daisies. Wire netting, secured in a plastic hair-spray top, provides the container, and this in turn is fixed by plasticine to a dish.

on my family once again. I fumed – and my poor husband really caught the brunt of it.

Depression and dissatisfaction gripped me. The independence of which I was so proud meant nothing. Again the question 'Why me?' raised its ugly head.

New discovery

At this point, a friend took me to her church – I had stopped going a long time ago – because she thought it would 'do me good', although I must say I had grave doubts on that score. The minister kept talking about the love of God for the individual. This was quite new to me and I came home and told my husband that to my surprise I had actually quite enjoyed the service. I attended church sporadically and as my body started to recover once again, we entered into a period of very happy family life.

God's love for the individual was, as I have said, a new idea for me. Even when thinking it over afterwards I could not grasp the complete significance of it. But one day the minister explained that God's love lay in Jesus Christ and that if we surrendered our life and will to him, he would make us free.

This really went against the grain! Surrender my regained independence and become a pawn! That was definitely not for me. But the word 'freedom' nagged at

me for a long time. Eventually I gave up the unequal struggle. I surrendered my will and independence to Jesus Christ – and I found freedom.

It sounds paradoxical to those who have not yet experienced the love of God. But it is true. It is freedom that works. The question 'Why me?' has never troubled me again. God may allow physical and spiritual setbacks. But it is for a good reason if only we will allow him to use them.

Care for detail

God taught me really to look and see the beauty he has given us: to study a daisy and wonder at the thought and care for detail that has gone into the design; or the magnificent bloom of a lily.

This love of detail is shown in infinite ways. In hot countries it can be seen in the chameleon's camouflage, or the cactus with inbuilt watersacs. There are trees which bear cones that will only open and seed if actually burnt by a flame, so that the seed falls to the ground and grows once the forest fires have passed over. The eagles care for their young in the inhospitable mountain peaks. The seeds of plants on the plains are distributed in a million ways. There are so many wonders all around us – not just to give us pleasure, but as examples of God's love and care and design in day-to-day living.

As the followers of Jesus gathered round him on the mountains of Galilee, he said: 'Look at the lilies! They

don't toil and spin, and yet Solomon in all his glory was not robed as well as they are. And if God provides clothing for the flowers that are here today and gone tomorrow, don't you suppose that he will provide clothing for you, you doubters? And don't worry about food – what to eat and drink; don't worry at all that God will provide it for you. All mankind scratches for its daily bread, but your heavenly Father knows your needs. He will always give you all you need from day to day if you will make the Kingdom of God your primary concern.'

'Eat up – it's good for you!'

Have you ever been completely at the mercy of your children? For a few weeks, some time ago, I lost the use of my right arm as well as my left, because of over-use through the years. I had the humbling experience of sitting at the table having food shovelled into my mouth with gleeful cries of 'Eat it all up, it's good for you!' At last the children could get one over on a bossy mother – and they decided to take full advantage. The spectacle of me trying to eat Italian spaghetti by sucking hard sent them all into hysterics and had them rolling on the floor!

My six-year-old daughter would come rushing home from school wanting to help me. The way she washed my hands and face put me to shame, she was so gentle. Eventually I was taken back to my parents to be lovingly looked after – though even my father had a gleam in his eye when he approached me with a spoon!

God showed his love for me in every detail. My husband and children were well looked after by our friends and were happy. I was given great peace of mind and happiness of heart and my parents the strength once again to cope.

As a result, the love of God and the reality of the presence of Jesus in my life is very real to me in day-to-day living. He is not there only for times of disaster and personal trials. He is there all the time, waiting to demonstrate his love, and waiting for us to acknowledge Jesus as our Lord and Saviour so that he can pour down all the blessings of a life made new and re-created – whether we be a humble daisy or a hybrid rose!

Making a start

Everyone must develop in their own way. I hope that this book will begin to show you some ways of expanding your personality in creative work with flowers. When you have the confidence of technical know-how you can begin to interpret different styles for yourself.

Principles of flower arrangement

People have been arranging flowers for many, many centuries. Wall-paintings hundreds of years old have been found showing flowers in vases. Although the popularity of flower arrangement has varied at different times, the art has never died out.

Different times – different designs

It is interesting to see how the favourite designs of a particular period reflect the general attitudes and conditions of society at that time. For example, in the reign of Elizabeth I flowers and foliage were mostly used to freshen and sweeten the atmosphere. The lack of sanitation and the misguided belief that fresh air was harmful made this essential! So aromatic flowers were strewn among the rushes on the floor. Bed-linen was sweetened with lavender. And when ladies went out, they wore posies or carried pomanders (oranges studded with cloves) to wave in front of their noses and make the foul air of the streets more bearable.

The Victorian era was quite different. The Victorians' love of knick-knacks, ponderous furniture, and rather formal and restricted family life is reflected in their use of flowers. They were fond of small posies and stiff, formal arrangements. It was also a very romantic age, and a gentleman would send a corsage to the lady of his choice. The 'language of flowers' was all the vogue. Each flower had a special symbolical meaning – roses for love; pansies for thought, and so on.

Earlier this century Constance Spry introduced a far more free and easy attitude to flower arrangement. She mixed colours and varieties of flowers with fruit and vegetables in a glorious profusion of colour, reminiscent of paintings by the old Dutch masters.

In our own so-called permissive age, the whole idea is to arrange flowers in the style that holds most appeal for you. But freedom must always be based on discipline, on the way things are designed, on the 'rules of the game'.

And of course, what holds good in the small world of flower arrangement applies to life in general. It is not just

Sharp scissors
Pinholders or needlepoints (or fakirs) in various sizes
One-inch diameter wire netting
Bucket
Composite blocks for holding flower stems. It comes in several sizes and shapes and can be cut to suit your containers. This brand is called oasis. It must be well soaked in water for two hours or so before use.
Gripfixholders for holding the blocks in place.

flowers that need attention to the basic rules to bring out the best in them. We need this ourselves for the whole of life. The Bible's rules for living give us the direction and support we need to prevent life being formless, aimless and purposeless. As individuals we all have a part to play in the rich pattern of life in this world.

So the main thing is to design your arrangement to fit in with the way flowers have been designed: not to bend them to artificial shapes, but to bring out the beauty and colour and form they express.

Useful equipment

Here are some of the basic requirements for simple flower arrangements. All of them can be bought at a good florist's or garden hardware shop.

Basic rules

Over the years many practical rules have been built up by experience. Here are some simple points for you to follow:

1. *Give your flowers and foliage a really good drink in deep water, preferably overnight.* This helps to ensure maximum nourishment before you arrange them. If the flowers are bought, recut the base of the stems and hammer woody ones. If you are gathering them from the garden, cut in the early morning or in the evening.

2. *Cut your flowers to different lengths when you begin using them.* Many people hate to cut stems, but it is essential if each bloom is to be seen.

3. *All flowers must spring from a central source.* If you remember that flowers grow from the centre of the bulb or root, it will help to make your arrangement look more natural.

4. *Use pointed flowers (e.g. buds, gladioli, foliage) to outline the arrangement.* This will give it delicacy.

5. *Use heavier flowers (e.g. roses, peonies) towards the middle.* These then fill in the outline.

6. *Bring the most strongly coloured flower into the centre.* In a bunch of mixed coloured flowers the white ones will take your eye, and so will the very dark ones. Make them important by bringing them well into the centre of the arrangement.

The flowers used in this arrangement are roses (Iceberg, Betina, Anna Wheatcroft), iris leaves, campanulas, variegated ivy, orange antirrhinum, blue delphinium, mock orange blossom, Hosta glauca, Hosta undulata, and prunus leaves. These are all garden flowers gathered from my own and from friends' gardens.

7. *The height of your largest flower should be at least one and a half times the height of your container.* This can be varied slightly of course, but it is important to keep a balance between the container and the flowers.

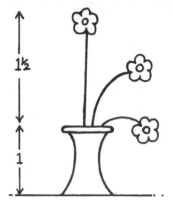

You can afford to be a little flexible about all these rules, except for the first one. Always remember that your flowers and foliage are the most important part of flower arrangement. We are not creating their beauty, merely enhancing it, so caring for them and letting them have their way is the most important consideration. No one has ever been able to persuade a left-curving branch to conform to their wishes for a right-curving arrangement. Even chatting it up doesn't help! So change *your* ideas. Somewhere in these chapters you should be able to find a shape that will show your flowers to advantage.

Containers

Perhaps the nearest you have got to flower arrangement is to take a bunch of flowers and plonk them into the nearest cut-glass vase. You may not think you are capable of doing anything more. Be a bit bolder. Take that tall cut-glass vase, give it a good scrub with vinegar water to make it sparkle, and put it somewhere where the light will reflect its full beauty – empty! Glass vases are not the easiest of containers to use when you are starting out.

Have a good hunt through your cupboards for containers that would suit the flowers you have. If you are using oasis or similar composition holding material make sure it is well soaked. If you are using wire-netting in a precious silver or china vase, be sure you line the vase with polythene.

Containers do not have to be expensive. As long as they are a good plain shape and sturdy enough to support the kind of flowers you have chosen, many household items can be used.

Here are some examples of the shapes and kinds of container that I have found most useful.

1. A loaf tin or rectangular dish. The tin can be lined with aluminium foil or polythene to prevent leaks, and painted a neutral shade.

2. A round bowl or tub.

3. A shallow dish – round, oval or rectangular.

4. An aluminium or plastic food container.

5. A pedestal vase.

6. A cup shape – either ceramic or plastic.

Expensive containers are not always necessary. This is a marmalade pot dipped in white emulsion paint and left to dry. I have put pebbles for economy's sake in the bottom of the pot, filled it with water and wedged in a piece of oasis composite to protrude about 1 inch above the edge. This allows for a downward flow of flowers.

Arrangements in the home

What makes a home? Home may be one room, a large house, a caravan or even a tent. It may be full of beautiful things, or only the bare necessities. But the really important thing is for it always to be a place where you and others can relax, feel welcome and be happy. This applies to a bed-sitter as much as to a house.

Whatever domestic chores may face you every day, try to make sure of just a few minutes when you can be yourself and express your creative ability for your own enjoyment and the pleasure of others.

Family life is part of God's good design for human society. But we are not meant to be selfish and exclusive about our homes and families. All that God gives us, he gives us to share with others. And flowers are one way of welcoming other people in outgoing love and care. A few fresh flowers arranged to show their full beauty will spell out the message of welcome as effectively (sometimes more effectively because they are less showy) than elaborate, stylized arrangements.

The kitchen

You may not think of the kitchen as the ideal place for a flower arrangement. But if, like me, you spend a good deal

A few Carlton roses, to match the stair carpet, are placed in a butter dish to provide an interesting diversion on the stairs!

This canework holder has a coffee jar with wire netting inside and is ideal for a wall hanging. A simple diagonal-type arrangement contains variegated ivy, leopard-bane, narcissus and euphorbia.

of your time hovering around the sink, why not have a simple arrangement on the window-sill? Or on the kitchen table round which so many families sit? One single flower in a small pot can add beauty to the most ordinary meal. If there is not much space, paint a glass jar and hang it by a string from a bracket on the wall. A few nasturtiums will brighten the darkest kitchen.

A glorious profusion of colour on the kitchen table is provided by these nasturtiums. They grow happily in poor soil or tubs and window-boxes. A candle makes even the sink more exciting. All material is held in wire netting.

The hall

Halls come in many shapes and sizes – long ones, dark ones, square or oblong – but they are most important. This is usually the first bit of the house a visitor sees. A vase of warm-coloured flowers, properly placed, will show at once the welcome you want to give.

If you have small children around, it is sometimes wise to put the flowers high up. Exploring fingers can pull a flower to pieces in a matter of seconds! So to save patience, time and tears, invest in a wall vase. You can buy vases at prices to suit every purse, and it is not always the most expensive ones that look best. Or you can use the kind of container I suggested for the kitchen wall.

Some staircases have a landing window. Flowers

Arrangement for a long dining-table

A painted bread tin, lined with polythene, holds crumpled wire netting fixed firmly to the sides of the tin. If the netting moves around, cut small pieces of the wire and bend them over the edges of the tin.

A is about 8 inches above the table and is the highest point of the arrangement.

B and C are as long as you wish to make them, but are the same length.

A is placed in the middle centre of the container and B and C protrude over the ends of the tin. Try to keep them as flat as possible.

D E F G are four equal lengths of flower or foliage. Place them on each side of B and C.

H and I are the widest part of the arrangement. Looking down at the outline you will see an oval. Fill in with shorter flowers, graduating them towards the outline, keeping it light and dainty. By constantly checking the shape from above, you will avoid creating a pudding effect. Remember that, to the person sitting down, the lower edges of the vase are visible, so do arrange some attractive flowers to curve gracefully towards the table.

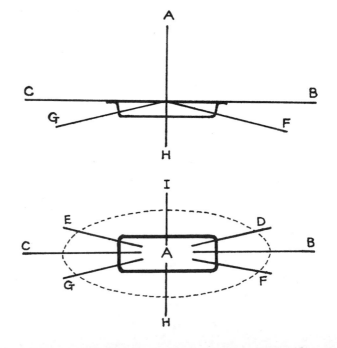

strategically placed on the sill will give constant pleasure, and make those interminable jaunts up and down stairs with youngsters less of a strain.

The living-room

This, of course, is the most important centre of family life and entertaining. Don't put too many arrangements in too many places, or the room will look like a florist's shop! But one or two good arrangements may even succeed in drawing eyes away from the television for a minute or two. A few flowers on a coffee table and a mantelpiece are usually sufficient. And if you are wanting a conversational evening, two or three candles will give the room a warm, intimate atmosphere and encourage people to feel happy and relaxed in your company. You know your guests, and what will appeal to them most.

If you are thinking of redecorating, it is a good idea to have one wall plain. Then you can show your flowers to the best advantage. If all your walls have a patterned paper, choose two or three bold flowers for a simple display.

Flowers on the table

A meal is always important, whether we eat in the kitchen or around the dining-table. But when it comes to flowers on the table, always remember one thing. Never make the arrangement too high. It does not help the conversation if you have to dodge round the flowers to see the person you are talking to!

A round bowl for a round table, a long bowl for a long table, is a rough rule-of-thumb guide. But practice will tell you what is the best shape to meet your particular requirements. And you will want to ring the changes.

Sometimes it is simpler to have one flower by every plate, rather than a formal centrepiece – a single rose-head floating in a small dish, for example. A lot depends on how many people there are and the amount of space.

There is no need to spend a great deal of money on all this. I have decorated three rooms with just ten daffodils. This is where a collection of 'accessories' – pretty stones and twigs, comes in useful. They help to make a little go a long way and this is particularly important in winter, when flowers have to be bought and are expensive.

The bedroom

You do not have to wait until you are ill to have flowers in the bedroom. The only time many husbands

If you have patterned wall-paper, try not to use too many varieties of flowers – it can look fussy. Two or three bold blooms in a simple style will give a more eye-catching effect.

and wives have to call their own is late at night. And a small vase of sweet-smelling flowers – lilies-of-the-valley, or freesias – and even a candle burning, can give the same relaxed, loving atmosphere as in the living-room. Again, you know best what is likely to appeal to your partner.

A stainless steel butter dish holds a pinholder with clematis Ville-de-Lyon and a few sweet peas. A candle completes this delicate arrangement.

Guests

Flowers in a guest-room always spell out a personal welcome. Sometimes it is necessary for our children to give up their rooms to visitors. If the owner of the bedroom is encouraged to arrange a few flowers on a dressing-table or by the bedside it will help the visitor to feel really welcome. Grandparents, for example, will sense that the room is lent willingly and with love.

An unexpected overnight guest may have to sleep on a studio couch or makeshift bed, but even this can look more interesting if you transfer a bowl of flowers from another room to place nearby.

Once, on holiday, we stopped for bed and breakfast at a place we had booked without seeing. It was a very old, cold, grey stone house, which looked most forbidding. But when we were taken inside, our spirits lifted. Big bowls of well-arranged flowers were everywhere. Suddenly it seemed the nicest place we had ever stayed in!

Flowers in hospital

Some time or another we all have to visit friends or relatives in hospital. It can be very expensive to buy flowers. There are so many calls on one's purse. And nurses are so overworked that they often don't have time to arrange all the flowers given to a patient.

One way round both these problems is to arrange a few flowers in a simple container before you go. This can be a real delight to the invalid, who will appreciate the flowers and, perhaps even more, the love you have shown by taking the trouble to arrange them. Sweet-smelling flowers (nothing too cloying) are a special pleasure. They do at least help to combat the antiseptic aroma of a hospital ward. You will find some more suggestions in the section on miniatures.

On one occasion when I had to go into hospital, I insisted on taking my own lilies-of-the-valley with me, much to the amusement of the nursing staff! But they were a great comfort to me, a real breath of home.

A bunch of flowers

Sometimes we are lucky enough to be given a bunch, or even a bouquet, of flowers. Then there is a great panic about what to do with them, and how to do it! Put them all in a bucket of water, to begin with, and really study their shapes and colours. There is no need to use them

A few tiny smiling-faced pansies placed in a water-filled eggshell in an egg cup will make a happy beginning to the day.

A liquid detergent bottle cut in half with a hot knife is covered with kitchen aluminium foil. A few stones are placed in the bottom for weight. A piece of oasis holds a few heads of delphinium, Cineraria maritima and a single head of a Madonna lily. This arrangement, including container, was made in ten minutes.

These flowers are rosebay willowherb — a weed! But how beautiful they can be, arranged in a simple fan shape. Their heads will curl to seek the light. If they begin to droop, add a little hot water to their container.

all in one huge arrangement. Make two or three, following the basic rules.

At the other extreme, we may have a bunch of wild flowers to deal with. These must be given a drink of warm water. Then they will last quite a while. The grasses can be dried off for use in winter.

If you are picking wild flowers yourself, make a point of taking one bloom only from each plant. If there is only one flower, resist the temptation, and leave it alone. God has given us a beautiful world and made us responsible for taking care of it. We have sadly neglected this responsibility all too often, and allowed God's world to be spoiled and polluted.

Wild flowers give so much pleasure. But indiscriminate picking by thousands of people spoils these things for everyone. So be sparing when you pick and never, never dig up the plants.

Don't be disheartened if your arrangements do not look the same as those in the photographs. Your flowers have their own character — all flowers have. For a start, their stems probably bend a different way. Try to see the finished arrangement in your mind and work to that, keeping in mind the basic rules of arrangement.

When you have finished, stand back and take a good long look. Do the flowers look comfortable sitting in their vase? Are there too many gaps? Is it well balanced for colour and shape? Above all, have you done justice to your flowers? If you are not entirely happy, don't fiddle too long, or you will bruise your blooms. Have another go another day, and before long you will have an arrangement that looks beautiful to you — and which makes your home a welcoming place.

Classic shapes

Basic shapes help to guide your hands and your eyes. They are outlines on which you can build your own designs and use your imagination to produce a very individual result.

The main shape is made first into a few flowers and then filled in towards the centre. Do not use too many flowers or the end result will be very heavy and solid. Aim for a natural appearance. It is better to use too few flowers than too many.

'L' shape

This flat dish contains a piece of oasis on a gripholder on the left of the dish. (Alternatively, a ball of crumpled wire netting fixed to a pinholder may be used.)

A and B are the same length. A is placed upright, two-thirds of the way back and left of the container. B flows out at right angles from the base of A. C is slightly shorter than A, and D shorter than C. E and F follow B in the same way. Graduate shorter flowers towards A D and C and towards B E and F.

All flowers spring from the base of A.

When completing your arrangement, insert some short and attractive flowers at the front base of A. This hides all the stem ends and creates a focal point.

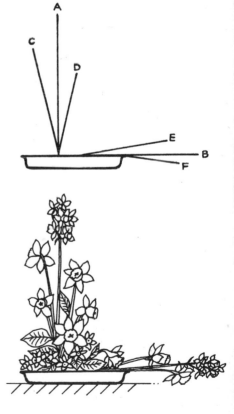

Flowers used are daffodils and narcissi.

Ball of flowers

Oasis protrudes ½ inch/1½ cms above container.
Take 9 flowers or pieces of foliage of the same length. Place A in the centre of the vase. 8 stems are then arranged straight into the sides of the oasis, like the spokes of a wheel. Begin to fill in the outline with different lengths of flowers. Watch the shape by looking down on the arrangement from above. A ball of flowers will begin to take shape. If a flower is too long it will become immediately

apparent. Keep pointed flowers or buds on the outline and heavier blooms lower, towards the centre of the ball.

Always cut your fill-in flowers to different lengths. Otherwise it will look like a ball of stems with flowers around the edge. Also large petalled flowers in a solid circle look heavy and clumsy.

Do not despair if the first time you try, the arrangement looks lopsided and you feel frustrated with it. Try again another day.

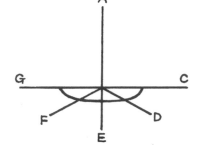

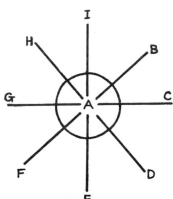

The arrangement here is of chrysanthemums, and I have used a candle for point A. Sweet peas, dianthus, sweet williams or wallflowers are very suitable for this design.

Fan

Seven straight stems of flowers and foliage create the outline. Use oasis or wire netting, protruding 1 inch above edge of vase. A B and C are the same length. Insert A two-thirds of the way centre back of the container. B and C are placed straight into the sides of the oasis or netting. Try to keep them as straight as possible, not emerging from the vase at an acute angle. D and E are slightly shorter than A and are placed at each side of the centre flower. G and F are very slightly shorter still and are inserted after D and E. H is placed last and provides a nice rounded front. These flowers are the basis of the fan. Keep the rest of your flowers shorter so that they do not spoil the outline.

Fill in with other blooms, remembering to cut them to different lengths, and use your most striking flower for low centre front as your focal point. Check the shape by looking at it sideways on. Try not to create a miserable caved-in appearance, but a full fronted beauty, proud of all its lovely flowers.

Flowers used here are dahlias, gladioli, cotoneaster and cornus foliage.

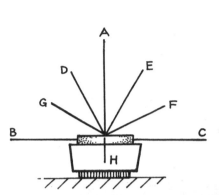

Diagonal

Oasis is used on a gripholder, protruding 1 inch above the vase.
A and B are the same length and are straight stemmed flowers. Insert A slanting right two-thirds back and to the right of the vase. Place B left front in a line with A. C D E and F are graduated towards A and B. Fill the outline with shorter flowers, varying the stem length, some angled towards A, others towards B. Create a focal point in the centre : in this instance it is the roses and grapes.
This particular arrangement looks attractive on a buffet table and contains Iceberg roses, scabious, sweet peas, dianthus and grapes.

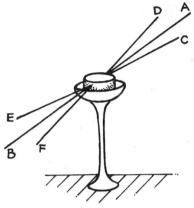

Crescent

This is an edged butter dish holding a piece of oasis. Any curved flowers are ideal for this arrangement (i.e. tulips, broom, roses). In this instance anemones are used.
A and B are the same length. Insert low into the oasis, at the ends of the dish. Encourage them to curve towards one another. C and D are slightly shorter, E and F shorter still, but all follow the same curving line as A and B. The centre is the lowest point. Try to visualise a new moon – this will indicate the line to follow.
One or two open flowers and some pretty foliage lie flat in the centre.
One bunch of short-stemmed anemones and a few pieces of foliage are all that is needed to complete this design, providing that you do not make A and B too long.

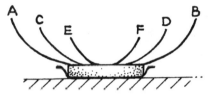

Directions for creating an oval shape are given on page 22.

Miniatures

You either love doing miniatures or you hate them. If you enjoy intricate needlework, then these are for you. If, on the other hand, you are one of those people – like me – who loathe sewing on buttons, this is your opportunity to tune your fingers and eyes to a new dimension.

For many years I was so used to creating arrangements on the grand scale that the charm of miniatures escaped me. However, an occasion arrived when it was necessary to experiment, and that was my undoing. I completely lost my heart to them. Miniature arrangements opened up a whole new world for me. For months I went around with my nose inches above the ground, marvelling at the tiny little flowers and leaves that had escaped my notice, and my scissors, before.

Flowers and containers

Two or three aubretia heads and dianthus foliage in a seashell make an arrangement fit for a queen. Two pieces of forget-me-not, with one or two miniature roses, have as much fascination for me now as a huge vase filled with all the prize blooms from a florist's shop. An added advantage is that it is very inexpensive to arrange miniatures. For example, you can use lilac stripped to single blooms, or one or two hyacinth florets. And the alpine section of a seed catalogue is full of flowers grown especially for the charm and grace of their tiny blossoms.

Begin by collecting mini-containers. This is number one priority. Empty lipstick holders, scent bottles, tiny doll's cups and saucers, salt and pepper pots, bottle tops, shells, thimbles – anything small can be called into service.

The method

To hold your flowers in place, use sand, tiny pebbles, moss, oasis, or even crumpled newspaper. If you have trouble holding the flowers, a pair of tweezers comes in useful, and nail scissors to cut the stems. Strip off all the leaves below the water line. Sometimes people find it difficult to push the stems into their holding agent, so an orange stick

A whelk shell containing a tiny piece of oasis, and filled with aubretia blooms and santolina foliage, adds a loving touch to a wrapped parcel. Use sticky tape to fix it to the wrapping-paper.

Left:
A lipstick holder takes on a new lease of life with santolina and dianthus foliage, cowslip heads, forget-me-nots and yarrow. Place a tiny piece of plasticine under the base of the container to ensure stability.

Right:
A shell with saxifrage, heath, scillas, forget-me-nots and silver birch foliage.

Left:
Lily-of-the-valley, tiny pieces of lilac, euphorbia heads, dianthus foliage, spiraea and weeping willow catkins are arranged in a fan shape on a flat salt dish, containing white 'flower fill' holding agent.

Right:
A tall gold bottle-top holds tiny pieces of azalea and wild crab-apple blossom.

Right:
A tiny doll's cup and saucer holds cupressus, saxifrage and heath. These are held in place with a crumpled hairpin.

Left:
An orange squash bottle-top takes on a more glamorous role here, holding dianthus foliage, erica, snow-in-summer, cupressus and crab-apple blossom.

or thin piece of twig is handy for making a hole into which you can then insert the flower stem. Soak your holding agent well. If your flowers need more water after a day or two, an eye-dropper is ideal for adding the extra liquid.

Follow the same rules in arranging miniatures as you would for larger designs. Don't take one rose, put it in a thimble, and think you have made a miniature arrangement. It may be pretty, but miniatures call for a little more imagination than this.

A few suggestions

A small arrangement is ideal for a patient in hospital.

A wrapped gift will look more interesting if a shell full of flowers is taped onto the outside.

A variety of flowers and containers on a tray for a convalescent little girl to arrange will keep her happy for a long time – and older people, too.

I once received a sardine-tin (well cleaned!) full of miniature roses and ericas in a variety of shades of pink. It was so sweetsmelling it gave me an enormous amount of pleasure. And I was so grateful for the care and love with which this little gift had been created.

With a little thought you will find all kinds of ways of using miniatures to satisfy your own creative urge and give pleasure to others.

A copper cauldron with a ball arrangement contains yarrow, aubretia, saxifrage and snow-in-summer.

The beauty of tiny things

There is nothing quite like getting down on our knees and really looking at a common, seemingly insignificant flower – a daisy or buttercup; wild thyme, bird's eye speedwell, scarlet pimpernel or trefoil. We tread these little flowers under foot whenever we walk across the grass in summer. And yet, when I look at them closely I can only marvel at the love and care God has lavished on these tiny things – the amazing detail of his creation. How then can I doubt his love and care for me? Hasn't he said that we are worth much more than the birds and flowers?

These beautiful miniature things are a permanent reminder that God loves us, no matter what we are like – with all our failures and inadequacies. The burden of worry and strain slips away as we look at the wild flowers, which God has clothed in greater finery than all King Solomon's glory. He knows all our needs. There is no need to wear ourselves out with worry and care. 'He will always give you all you need from day to day if you will make the Kingdom of God your primary concern.' And that's a promise!

A miniature copper kettle contains privet, snow-in-summer, euphorbia heads and leaves, yarrow, spiraea, silver birch catkins and a kerria head.

Dried flowers and collages

Here is another whole new area that can become a complete hobby in itself. Once you begin on flower arranging, there is just so much scope, so many ways to use your gifts and express yourself. I find myself echoing the Psalmist's words, 'O Lord, what a variety you have made! And in wisdom you have made them all! The earth is full of your riches.'

Materials

How many of us, when clearing the flower-beds in the latter part of the year, just cut back the shrubs and perennials and throw the cuttings on the compost heap? But these prunings are treasures in themselves.

Seed-heads are fascinating. Dianthus heads are like little bells and can be kept back for painting at Christmas. Delphinium and foxglove heads, and many, many others, depending on your locality, can be preserved and used for winter decorations and collages.

Search the hedgerows for grasses and heads of wild clematis (old man's beard). If you live in a built-up area, this is the time to look for fallen twigs, and invest in a trip to greener parts. You shouldn't have to go too far to find fresh leaves.

Many flower seeds produce blossoms which are called everlasting flowers: helichrysum, helipterum, rhodanthes, and so on. These seeds can be bought from any good seed merchant. Grown in the garden, they produce a great many flowers which can cheer a dark room all through the winter.

If you decide to buy seeds and grow your own everlasting flowers and grasses, why not get your friends to join in? By sharing the packets of seed, or pooling the flowers when grown you can all get a much greater variety. This is particularly useful if you have not much space. And sharing is a lot more fun than doing things on your own. If you still find you have grown more than you need, offer them to someone who cannot grow their own.

These seed-heads, flowers and grasses are arranged in the same way as fresh material, and may be inserted in sand,

A twig covered in lichen – collected on holiday – is a pretty background for three daffodils. A selection of attractive stones covers the pinholder in the flat dish.

oasis, or any substance which is sold specifically for dried flower work. Choose a container which will balance your arrangement, and which can be kept in use all winter.

Accessories

Of course there are a great many other materials you can collect and use for dried flower arrangements and collages. Rocks, pebbles, pieces of wood and shells can all be used. It is really worth while looking out for as many attractive samples of these as you can find. It is an all-the-year-round interest. Holidays are an ideal time for collecting. You can come back with something to remind you of places visited. If friends going abroad know your interest, they may bring you something special. In ways like these you can build up a good collection of stones and shells. And with just two or three flowers, a piece of bark and a few stones, you can create a really attractive arrangement – one which has the added advantage of lasting a long time. Only the flowers need to be changed.

It need not stop there. Twisted pieces of tree root are a real find. These may be cleaned in a mixture of household bleach and water, scraped clean with a knife, and either left white or given a thorough brushing with brown shoe polish. This will bring out natural highlights. Never use a high gloss varnish, as it destroys the texture. But you can use varnish to enhance the colour of shells and certain rocks that are found near water.

Beech leaves, three yellow tulips and chicks are arranged in a small plastic ice-cream dish on a moss-covered pinholder and put into a piece of cork bark.

The more you really study the look, feel and environment of your 'accessories', the more effectively you can bring out their innate beauty. This is just one little way of showing the respect and appreciation God expects us to give his created world. If each of us as individuals had this kind of attitude to the environment, the problems of pollution would soon be solved!

Methods of drying

There are various methods of drying fresh material. The hints set out here are merely a guide. I have not had the opportunity to try out all the substances that are now manufactured for drying flowers, and there may well be alternatives or short-cuts. But I have found the following methods satisfactory and economical.

Grasses. Cut before the seed ripens. Then hang in a bunch in an airy, moisture-free room or cupboard (an airing cupboard is a little too hot). This method will keep your grass stems straight. But if you want to give them a more natural curve, arrange them in a container and allow them to bend over the edges.

Fresh leaves. Beech, oak, holly, laurel, ferns, and so on can

A pretty shell has a piece of dry white container material pushed into the corner, in which are arranged rhodanthes, pink poker statice, eryngium heads, lavender, and Ammobium grandiflorum.

This is a preformed cone of oasis used dry. If these are unobtainable one may be carved from a block of the material. Purple xerantheums, harestail grass, eryngium and statice heads are used. Starting from the top, make small holes with an orange-stick and push the stems well into the material. Cover the cone completely, keeping the outline clear. Place the arrangement on a flat dish or a pedestal vase. For a complete change of colour – experiment with dried beech leaves, plastic berries, honesty or chinese lanterns (Physalis).

all be used. Cut before they turn colour, or while the sap is still rising. Hammer the ends of the stems and place them in a mixture of one-third glycerine and two-thirds hot water and allow them to drink this. The leaves will appear slightly oily when they are ready for removal. If they are left too long, they will become very greasy and be inclined to mildew. If your leaves look somewhat sad and bedraggled while in the mixture, remove and recut the stems, reheat the mixture and start again.

It is worth experimenting with many varieties of leaves. Some–such as eucalyptus–remain grey. Others turn shades of fawn and brown. Pussy willow will take on a slight sheen. All make good background material.

Wild and cultivated clematis. These have beautiful spiral seed-heads. Strip off all leaves. Then they respond very well to the glycerine treatment, turning shades of brown.

Everlasting flowers. I have put these under a general heading, because there are so many varieties. The general rule here appears to be that the more you cut, the more the plant produces. The flowers may be treated in the same way as grasses, by hanging them up to dry. What I usually do is take down the kitchen curtains and hang the flowers by wire ties from the curtain runners, leaving a window slightly ajar (while I'm at home!). But sun will fade the flowers a little. A spare room, cool passage or attic would also be suitable. On average, two weeks should be enough to dry the flowers. Then store in plastic bags until you are ready to use them.

Helichrysum heads should be cut before they are fully open, and placed in flat containers to dry. They can be mounted on wire for arrangement.

Seed-heads will be practically dry already if you pick them in late summer. I give these a light spray with polyurethane varnish, or a good spraying of hair lacquer, if the seed-heads are very delicate.

Hydrangeas. These are useful flowers and hold their colour well. Arrange them in a vase containing an inch or two of water. They will drink what they need and then dry off quite naturally.

Borax treatment for single flower-heads. Cut the flowers when they are young. Cover the bottom of a cardboard box with a three-inch layer of borax (obtainable from any chemist). Place the flower-heads face down in the box, separate from one another, and cover completely with more borax. Put the box in a warm cupboard – an airing cupboard is fine. In the case of delicate, light-textured flowers, such

This is a piece of wood, found by Guy on the way home from school. A tiny piece of oasis is glued on to the wood and a selection of grasses is arranged in this. A snail shell also glued to the wood and filled with dry oasis holds santolina flowers and Ammobium grandiflorum, flowing in a natural line down the wood.

Dried grasses, pink poker statice, glycerined clematis heads, pink and white helipterums, white xerantheums, knapweed, rhodanthes and cones are arranged in wire netting to make an attractive display for the winter months.

as pansies, clematis, cosmos, daffodils, narcissi, violets, cornflowers and young fern fronds, check progress after thirty-six hours. Gently brush aside the top layer of borax, and if the flowers feel dry to the touch remove them carefully. Heavier-textured flowers, such as roses, gladioli, stocks, marigolds, carnations and some lilies should be ready in a week.

All flowers will retain their colour, but you need to watch them carefully while they are being treated. If they are left in the borax too long they will deteriorate. Wire the heads with light-grade wire on to false stems for arrangement purposes.

Berries and gourds can be preserved if you keep the air from them by painting them all over with clear varnish.

Never be afraid to experiment. Nearly everything is trial and error. We learn from our mistakes until we perfect our own particular method, the one that suits our requirements best. There are some excellent books on dried flower arrangement. Once you have discovered how interesting it can be, it is worthwhile finding out more about the subject.

Small arrangements are greatly appreciated as gifts. Little shells, small plastic containers and painted glass pots can all be pressed into service for present-making at birthday and Christmas time. And dried flowers and materials offer endless scope for table and other seasonal decorations.

Another way of using dried materials is to make collages.

Decorative tree

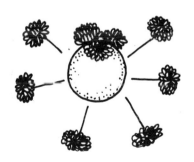

Take a dry, medium-sized preformed oasis ball or cut one from a block.
Cut the stem off the helichrysum and pierce the head with a long pin, pushing it well into the ball, until it is covered completely. Make sure you keep the round outline. When the ball is nearly complete, push one end of a $\frac{1}{2}$ inch diameter dowelling rod about twelve inches long into the base. Take a yoghurt or cream carton and fill with sand. A paper doily, with a hole in the centre, covers the top of the carton. Another doily is pinned round the carton. Push the other end of the dowelling rod through the top doily and into the carton. The sand will hold it in place. A few helichrysum

heads pinned into the doily, and ribbons pinned under the ball, complete this ball-tree. This can be made in an evening.
An alternative to the tree is to complete the ball. Using two long hairpins, wire a piece of ribbon into the ball and hang it from the ceiling.

These are an art in themselves and deserve a special section of their own.

Collages

Collages have recently become very popular. But they are expensive to buy – so why not have a go at making your own? You do not need a lot of costly materials.

Soon there will be no holding you. Before you know where you are you will have become adept at making anything from a three-inch miniature, complete with calendar, to a six-foot collage for the living-room wall!

You can use all kinds of things to make a collage – flowers, seed-heads, little pieces of bark, lichen, cones, tiny stones. If you collect these things when you go away, you can create a special collage that will always remind you of a happy holiday.

It can become a fascinating hobby, one which handicapped as well as more active people can enjoy. I know of one lady who, although she is confined to a chair and suffers from loss of sensitivity and stiff joints in her hands, immensely enjoys making these collages. It can be a new, creative hobby when knitting and needlework are impossible. If you enjoy it yourself and are able to collect more materials than you need, look around for someone who is unable to get about. You may be able to open up whole new horizons in an otherwise dull and monotonous existence.

Little things like this may seem unimportant. But it is in just such simple, thoughtful, caring, sharing ways that ordinary people can follow the example of Jesus and obey

You will need:

Small scissors
Thick card – white or coloured
Cloth, if required – hessian or velvet is good
A good clear glue
Tweezers
Coloured cord
Some dried flowers, leaves, grasses, etc.

Framed picture

Cover a piece of card with cloth (velvet or hessian makes a good background). Squeeze glue on the face and edges of the card. Cover the glued card with the cloth, smoothing it to remove the wrinkles. Turn the card over. Snip the corners of the cloth, glue all the edges, and stick them down. Cut a piece of paper the same size as the card and stick it firmly into place over the edges of the cloth to neaten the back. Then make your collage design as before. Be very sparing with the glue. When you are really pleased with the results, they can be framed and even glassed.

his instruction to 'love each other just as much as I love you. Your strong love for each other will prove to the world that you are my disciples'. And in obeying his commands we also prove that our love for him is real.

Collage calendars

Take a piece of fairly stiff card. Punch two holes top centre, and insert your cord for hanging. Make two slits lower down, to hold the calendar block.

Take a piece of paper the same size as your card. Study your flowers and other materials you have collected to make the collage. Then create and draw a rough design on the paper. The pictures show the sort of designs you could use.

Now take the card and lay out the outline of your design in flowers or grasses. Keep it as flat as possible. And follow the same principles as for fresh flower arranging – light, pointed material on the outside; heavier flowers towards the centre.

Do not stick your stems on top of one another. Cut them with

your scissors and drop a little glue along the back of the stem and flower. Place gently but firmly into the selected position. Bring your most eye-catching bloom into the centre, cutting the stems right down to the base. Fill in with little pieces of flowers and foliage, using the tweezers if necessary. Continue in this way until the design is completed.

Colour

I need colour in my own home – especially in the kitchen! The sight of some gleaming yellow paintwork makes me feel – and work – much better. It stops me looking wistfully out into the sunlit garden when I should be cooking supper!

We all need colour in some form or another and this is now being recognized by psychiatrists around the world. Plain cream walls no longer predominate in our hospital wards. Many dark dreary waiting-rooms are taking on a new lease of life. And interior decorators give us instructions in magazines on how to make our homes more beautiful with colour.

We all react in some way to colour. Excitable people need the quietening effect of the cool, calm hues, such as violet, blue and green. Placid people require the stimulation of warm hues, red, yellow and orange. Most of us like a good mixture of both. This is a very general statement, but you can see how colour can affect our personality and mood. Can you imagine what it would be like living in a bright red room – ceiling, walls, furnishings, all red? Our eyes would ache. A vase of cool green leaves would be very welcome.

When we think of a colour we may 'see' it in a variety of ways. Take green, for example. There is the fresh spring green of a leaf, the dark green of holly, the yellow-green of privet, or catkin green. There are so many tints, shades or tones. If you go to buy a tin of green paint there is a bewildering choice on the sample card.

A vase of white flowers is not plain and uninteresting. By looking at each flower carefully, you will see that every petal varies very slightly in shading. Each colour has its own 'colour-value' – the degree to which it attracts your eye. One yellow daffodil is more obvious than two mauve anemones. One orange tulip has better decorational value than one blue iris. So if you have a small amount of money to spend on flowers choose the bright warm colours.

Using colour to good effect

Should you choose flowers to match your room? Up to a point, yes. Country cottages which nestle into their

A lovely mixture of cornus, light and dark pink tulips, orange polyanthus, two heads of Amaryllis lily, an orange gerbera and coleus leaves, give a glow to any room. Study the colour grouping here.

surroundings need unsophisticated, uncontrived posies of flowers. If you are a collector of beautiful porcelain, flowers with dainty colours – like sweet peas – should be used near the display cabinets. If you are putting flowers in a living-room, pick up the colour of a cushion or curtains for an uncluttered over-all effect. Do not be afraid to experiment. A slightly cold-looking blue room can be brought to life with a bowl of orange marigolds or gladioli. The colours complement one another. Pinky-mauve flowers on a mid-brown table may be restful, but they are rather uninteresting. Neither enhances the other. You will learn as you go along, and if like me you make some catastrophic mistakes, never mind, you will steer clear of them in future.

When you are arranging a bowl of mixed coloured flowers, place the colours in groups, taking the most brilliant or darker colour into the centre. But there is one point to watch for. When you look at a vase from a distance, a very dark flower can give the impression of a hole in the centre of the arrangement. So place light foliage behind it to bring the flower into prominence. It is possible to avoid a spotty effect by inserting all the flowers of one colour before beginning on the next. When you position your outline, try to imagine which way each colour will sweep down through the arrangement.

To my eyes, no flower clashes with another. You can put one colour with another which in a dress fabric would probably set your teeth on edge. Experiment with dominant colours such as red and purple, using a little grey foliage. Grey tones down the visual impact, creating a more harmonious effect and avoids spots before the eyes.

A blue arrangement is very beautiful, but the colour absorbs light, so be careful about using it in a dark room. Position it so that light from a window shines directly on to it, and the flowers will be greatly enhanced.

Flats, houses in towns, and old period houses with small windows all suffer badly from dark corners. This is where all the rainbow colours of flowers come into their own. A bowl of golden rod, rudbeckia or daffodils will give the impression of sunlight. Orange marigolds, poppies, geraniums, orange alstromeria will fill you with the warmth of a sunset.

Light

If it is at all possible, invest in a small directional light which may be moved to shine directly on to your flowers, making the arrangement a focal point in the room. This can also apply to potted plants grouped for effect. Light is the frame of a flower arrangement, it enhances the colour

Beautiful blues and lilacs combine to rest the senses and present a feeling of tranquillity. A lilac gladioli, freesias, tulips and stocks are arranged with blue Dutch iris, forget-me-nots, lungwort and grey Cineraria maritima.

A diagonal arrangement of leaves only. Harts-tongue, Hosta undulata, bergenia-vinca, berberis, gardener's garters, Cineraria maritima and strawberry leaves.

and texture. Without it, even the most glowing colours may seem drab and uninteresting. A new dimension has come into our lives recently by installing, outside our sitting-room window, an external wall light which illuminates both plants and trees near the house.

The effect is rather like looking at a colour slide through a projector. The surrounding darkness is a dramatic contrast to the variety of colours in the plants. Many people, seeing our garden by night, have been amazed at the delicate and beautiful variety of greens. We have one single light, the type used on building sites, which consumes a relatively small amount of electricity. The cost is repaid a hundred times over by the beauty which is unfolded at night time.

Tones and shades

One of my own favourite arrangements uses just green leaves. Each is different from the others in colour, shape and texture. If you are selecting from a garden or woodland, choose each one as you would a flower, and build up a composition as a floral arrangement. There are tones and shades galore; blue-green, yellow-green, brown-green, red-green – so many and so beautiful. To begin with, use single leaves or small branchlets only, rather than whole branches, and wait for the compliments to pour in! Often leaves are regarded as fillers rather than things of beauty in their own right.

While we are talking about colour – a word on containers. Choose a vase to match your most dominant hue, or alternatively use neutral shades. These are safe and you can use them again and again.

Although it has been given us free to enjoy, colour is extremely valuable. Let's make the most of it and be grateful that we are surrounded with such an abundance of colour that we can pick and choose whatever suits our mood.

Flowers in towns

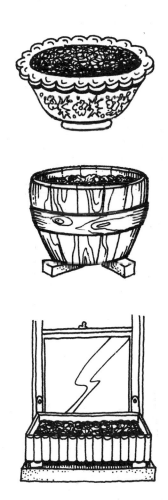

If you have the creative urge and want to grow things for your arrangements, don't let lack of space put you off. There are many ways of getting round the problem. Inexpensive containers are marketed for just this very purpose. And it is possible with a little thought to provide your own material at most times of the year.

Tubs and pots

Place a few broken crocks in the bottom to allow for drainage. Some tubs which you can make yourself – out of old wine casks cut in half, for example – need holes drilled in the bottom to facilitate drainage. It is useful to place the tub on bricks to encourage better drainage – or on castors, so that you can move it easily. To prevent the soil from turning sour, again use a well-soaked potting compost and fill three-quarters full before planting in the same way as for the baskets. There is an immense variety of plants, bulbs and shrubs available. Bulbs should be dressed occasionally with a little bone meal. And some plants – e.g. rhododendrons – need peat mixed with the compost.

I have seen people use all sorts of objects never intended to hold plants – old hip-baths, sinks, washbasins, wheelbarrows, and so on. And all these have been used with success. The essentials are good drainage, good soil, watering, and a little liquid manure occasionally. If holes cannot be drilled in the base of the container, be certain that there is a good layer of broken crocks at the bottom. You can use old flower pots, etc. and perhaps a few pieces of charcoal to keep the soil sweet. It is possible to create a miniature rock garden using alpine plants. What scope this gives for miniature arrangement addicts!

Window-boxes

Colourful window-boxes cheer many city streets, and once installed are very easy to maintain. Boxes can be made of wood – red cedar, teak, oak, elm – lined with zinc or a light metal, or painted inside and out with a preservative which after drying out is harmless to plant roots. Other boxes can be bought ready-made in other materials such as artificial stone, concrete, metal or plastic. These of course need very little maintenance.

Be certain that your box is held very firmly in position on your outer window-sill, using very strong metal brackets. Place it on small blocks of wood so that the rain does not collect underneath and rot the sill. When in position, spread a good layer of crocks at the bottom, placing one large piece over each drainage hole. Then add a few pieces of charcoal, a layer of moss and leaves and good potting compost. Use upright plants and a few trailing ones to gain maximum effect. Water weekly or more frequently in hot weather, including a liquid manure every two weeks.

One very cheap container is a wine or cordial bottle. A

These few French marigolds and three small pelargonium heads were grown in a window-box. Here they have been picked and arranged in oasis on a butter dish. A small brass or copper dish would serve equally well. Placed where sunlight falls on them they can add a splash of brilliant colour to a city room.

coloured glass one is the most effective. Fill three-quarters full with well-soaked potting compost and top it up with a little peat. Lay it on its side and drill a hole in the base about 1 inch in diameter. Insert a pelargonium cutting through the hole and into the soil and leave it until it has made roots. Tie a piece of strong twine round the neck of the bottle and hang it from a bracket on the outside wall. Water it from the top. Make sure it can't hit the wall and break when the wind blows.

There are so many flowers and shrubs available that it is worth while seeking the advice of a good nursery or seedsman. Tell them whether you live in a sooty city, or have to contend with salty air by the coast, or high winds. Then they will recommend the best plants for your area. After all, gaps in a window-box where plants have died are going to be far more noticeable than in a large garden. It is also worth telling them that you are interested in

flower arrangements. Then they can suggest plants that flower profusely.

Hanging baskets

These take little space – though remember to hang them high enough to avoid knocking your head! It is better to have your basket too large than too small. That way you can make sure there is enough soil for your plants to flourish.

Thickly line your basket with fresh damp moss. Then fill halfway with a good potting compost. Insert your plants – two or three large ones in the centre, with smaller trailing varieties around the edge and between the larger plants. Fill to the top with more compost, firming it gently around the roots, and leave a slight depression in the centre. Soak the whole basket thoroughly by placing it in a bath or sink of water. Allow the surplus water to drain off before hanging up the basket.

Baskets are inclined to dry out fairly quickly, so in very hot weather check daily. If possible immerse in a bath of water, adding a little liquid manure once every two weeks while the flowers are coming into bud.

Pot plants

Plants grown for the beauty of their leaves are tremendously important. Begonia rex in its different shadings, coleus and variegated ivy, for example, yield just that extra colour and texture when needed. Again pick carefully. Avoid growing shoots and take only the mature leaf. Chlorophytum shoots may be cut off, used in an arrangement and replanted afterwards. There is sometimes an added bonus. Leaves that have been in water for some time often grow roots of their own. So inspect before throwing them out. You may have another pot plant on the way!

One last point to mention. Children love growing things. They enjoy looking after small cuttings and bringing them to maturity. Yet so often we do not think beyond growing mustard and cress on a piece of flannel. They get tremendous satisfaction out of planting pips and watching them grow into orange, lemon or peach trees. To avoid disappointment, though, it's a good idea to tell them that it is unlikely the trees will bear fruit. But a chestnut or an acorn will flourish when put in a permanent position, and will teach them to value the miracle that turns a small seed into a magnificent tree.

Most children love messing about with water and earth and getting themselves thoroughly grubby. Encourage them to use their imagination by allowing them to plant their

A few sprays of free-flowering fuchsia and double petunias grown in a garden tub add warmth and beauty to any room. Do not forget to hammer the woody stems of the fuchsia and give them a good drink well before arranging them.

own gardens or tubs. Teach them how to care for and maintain their flowers. And let them also learn to clear up after themselves!

The natural world is full of everyday miracles. It is not only children who stop and wonder at the way a brown, dried-up seed can grow into a beautiful new flowering plant, or a pip into a great tree. It makes us pause and marvel at the power of the One who designed our world, and his infinite patience and care for detail. Jesus once described the kingdom of God – the family of all those who love and follow him – in these words: 'It is like a tiny mustard seed! Though this is one of the smallest of seeds, yet it grows to become one of the largest of plants, with long branches where birds can build their nests and be sheltered.' There is room in God's kingdom for everyone – no matter how old or how young.

When all your hard work is rewarded with a riot of colour, pick carefully – a flower here, a leaf there. Make them seem more important by using a few of the accessories you have collected during the year – a piece of driftwood, lichen, or a few stones. You will achieve a tremendous sense of satisfaction: colour outside your home to cheer passers-by, and colour inside to warm your heart. In some of our drab cities we can wage our own private war on pollution.

Charlotte with a young lemon tree grown from a pip.

Special occasions

As you become more practiced in the art of arranging flowers, you are bound to be called upon to use your talent more widely. There are always occasions which flowers can help to make something special and this is a lovely way to share the beauty of God's creation with others.

Flowers in church

You may well be asked to arrange flowers in church. Many people pale at the thought! All kinds of questions arise. 'Am I good enough?' 'How much will it cost?' 'What will the congregation think of my efforts?' None of these points should stand in your way. By learning the basic rules of arrangement you cannot go far wrong. Lack of money need not be a stumbling-block. A large vase can be filled effectively with greenery – laurel, privet or dried grasses and a few flowers. And although you obviously want to please the congregation, who are you doing the flowers for? First and foremost you are doing them for God. He knows that you want to please him and show your love for him to the best of your ability.

Many churches are ill-equipped with containers. Tall thin glass vases abound! Cheap plastic dishes are a worth-while investment. Some churches have one person to organize a flower rota. This spreads the privilege around many people. In my own church, after the Sunday evening service the flowers are taken down, arranged in cellophane bags and delivered – with a note from our minister – to anybody we know who is ill, bereaved or lonely. The job of taking the flowers is usually left to the person who has provided and arranged them. It is wonderful to see the pleasure of those who receive the bouquets.

If you have to buy flowers for Christmas, Easter, weddings and so on, do warn the florist at least a week beforehand, particularly if you are ordering special colours or blooms. This gives him a chance to look around the market so that he can tell you what will be available. Order them for the day before the occasion, so that the flowers can have a good drink. If you are using oasis – soak it well. For Christmas, don't limit yourself to a few white chrysanthemums in a

A flat dish is used for this diagonal arrangement. Three candles of varying lengths are inserted first into oasis pushed on to a pinholder. Add the carnations in a sweeping line – adding pink baubles, cyclamen and cloryphytum plantlets for a low focal point.

If you have a limited choice of colour, flowers and money, use pale backing material. In this instance cow parsley and wild crab-apple blossom.

The container is a typical altar vase.

To produce the effect here I have used four metal cones (illustrated opposite), pushed firmly into the oasis and wire netting, filled with water and holding the branches. This is a way of adding extra height.

This arrangement is suitable for a small church, but is too delicate for a larger building.

Do try to arrange for someone to top up the cones and vase with water regularly.

The flowers used here are twelve small carnations, ten tiny tulips, five short stocks, cow parsley, crab-apple and bergenia leaves.

vase. Try to be a little more imaginative. Easter calls for a riot of colour to express our joy that Christ has triumphed over death. At weddings, the bride usually specifies the colour of the flowers. Some of the women in the church may well feel that they would like to arrange the flowers for the bride, making a personal contribution to a happy and memorable day.

Large displays may seem frightening to attempt but really they are only bigger versions of all the outlines shown on previous pages.

Churches vary enormously. I have used three different examples for various occasions. If your church has stained-glass windows, do not try to compete with their glorious colours. Either pick out one of the rich tones and build around that, or use neutral or pastel shades. If the building is dimly lit, avoid any of the blue tones, as they are inclined to merge with the background. In a small, plain church the flowers will be visible to all. If you want to put flowers on the pulpit, ask the minister first. He may use his arms to emphasize a point and feel inhibited if the flowers are dangerously close. Wall vases are useful, particularly if the church has a gallery. People upstairs may then also enjoy the arrangement. It may be necessary to stand on

a chair to arrange the vases, if they are fixed. But others are removable, so you can arrange them at a more comfortable level.

A few churches have little niches on either side of the altar. These can be used to great effect. Again, keep the flowers as flat as possible. Otherwise you will have your heart in your mouth all through the service, whenever the minister or altar boys brush past! If you are ever asked to do the flowers at a church you are not familiar with, try to attend a service beforehand so that you know what situations can be used to best advantage. By sitting quietly after the service you can absorb the atmosphere and feel of the building.

Christmas

There are many times during the year when we decorate our homes for special occasions. The first that comes to mind is Christmas. It is worth planning for this festival throughout the year. I previously mentioned the seed-heads from the flower-beds and collecting teasels and pieces of

Metal cone vases, very useful for tall arrangements in churches and larger buildings.

A fan arrangement for a traditional Christmas vase. Fill in the outline and then place your candle in the required position. If you want to light the candle, keep it well away from the flowers and holly. A few baubles placed in the centre complete this display.

My children call this a 'Gonk'. Crumple some ½ inch/2 cm wire netting into the shape of a cone with an open base. Make sure it stands firm and straight on its base and push small pieces of cupressus or other small-leaved evergreen into all the holes of the netting, completely covering it. Tiny baubles hooked through hairpins are then pushed into the greenery. Simple for children to make.

A cakeboard is the base for this table centre. Cones are glued in a star fashion to the board and others glued on top in a circle. Spray the whole arrangement with gold, silver or white paint, and glitter liberally. Place a small candleholder in the hole in the middle, insert a coloured candle and arrange a few baubles around the cones.

bark on summer walks. Buy cans of gold, white or silver paint and glitter before present-buying starts. Store all these bits and pieces carefully – perhaps in a box under the bed! Then you will have everything to hand when the time comes.

When using sprays, do cover everything close to hand with newspapers. On one memorable occasion I managed to redecorate the kitchen table, refrigerator and floor with gold. I felt I had the Midas touch! But it took hours to clean off. Have a window slightly open because of the fumes. Sprinkle with glitter when the paint is slightly tacky. Yoghurt and cream cartons, tin cans, wine bottles and so forth look entirely different when painted, and can be used to hold quite exotic arrangements.

You may be asked to be in charge of arranging the church flowers for a special occasion such as Christmas. This is an important job and one that you will want to do as well as possible. It is well worth doing, as the decorations contribute a great deal to the sense of occasion. They create a warm, colourful, welcoming atmosphere, and show our delight and

Church flowers at Christmas

Holly balls hang from the ceiling bars. As well as coloured baubles, they have yellow chrysanthemums inserted into the oasis to add colour. On the pulpit are simple ball arrangements on pedestal vases with hanging trails of ivy, using yellow spray chrysanthemums, variegated greenery, artificial holly berries and candles which may be lit.

The communion table and window-sills repeat the colour scheme in long, low fan arrangements. The larger display by the door is a free fall pedestal outline using masses of greenery and berried holly, yellow chrysanthemums and candles. The red-cellophaned glass-jars on the pulpit hold candles which, when lit, enhance the red banners.

Flowers for a wedding

Very few of these flowers were purchased from a shop. Generous friends allowed me to cut what I needed from their garden shrubs. The proteus will be given to the bride, and when dried will be a memento of her wedding day.

Two large pedestal arrangements in a sweeping diagonal shape contain rhododendrons, azaleas, camellias, roses, tulips, antirrhinum, acer, proteus and magnolias.

The bowls on the pulpit echo the line and contain star-of-the-veldt, azaleas and freesias.

The communion table holds a crescent, linking the two diagonal arrangements and using similar blooms.

enjoyment of the beauty of God's creation. Do not let the prospect daunt you too much. Stick to simple, bold arrangements, and you won't go far wrong.

The arrangements on the opposite page were done for my own church last Christmas. They are all larger editions of those made for use at home.

Easter

Easter is a glorious time when we celebrate the death and resurrection of Jesus Christ and should be a time of great rejoicing and happiness. One way of communicating what

Tree bark forms the base of this arrangement. Three chocolate Easter eggs are attached to the wood with plasticine. A small glass dish behind the eggs holds toning colours of freesias and polyanthus.

Five tulips and freesias arranged in a plastic trifle dish (wire wool will clean away the print). A few pebbles are used in the base for extra weight.

Easter means to us is in our homes, using eggs and fluffy chicks to depict the new life which is available to us. Depending on where you live, there should be sufficient flowers of various species to enable you to share the Easter message in a simple arrangement.

Parties

If you are having a party – do remember to place your flowers well out of the way of people brushing past. Stand your vase on a tall table in a corner, where it can be seen. But be careful not to have too many stems jutting forward, or these will be knocked about. Teenage parties can be a real challenge to your ingenuity – and your stamina! But a small arrangement of fruit, vegetables and flowers will give you quite a reputation as a way-out Mum!

Fruit and vegetables have a beauty of their own. Purple sprouting broccoli, aubergines, beetroot leaves, feathery carrot tops, fresh green and white celery heads, and chillies are just a few examples. Tomatoes, nuts, apples, oranges, mushrooms and so on may be mounted on orange sticks and together with some flowers make quite a stunning combination. Use all the materials as though they are flowers – each to be individually arranged. It might be wise to leave out the grapes – or you are bound eventually to find your arrangement half-eaten! Keep the grapes for a slightly more sophisticated adult party.

Birthdays, anniversaries and the arrival of new babies are all happy times. What better way of sharing our love than by giving flowers? With a little imagination, it is possible to make a really attractive arrangement created especially for the person we have in mind.

Easter in church

This is a very small church and large displays of flowers would be out of place. The curving lines of the tulips, magnolias, freesias and purple broccoli leaves and the simple oval flowers express the joy and simplicity of Easter. Provided that the magnolia stems have been split and given a good drink, they will last for three or four days in a cool church.

The gift of flowers

The past few years have been exciting ones for me, as invitations to demonstrate and speak about flower arrangement have increased. Through teaching at evening classes I have had the joy of seeing people's eyes gradually opened to the natural beauty of the world around them and to the possibility of using their own skill to display that beauty to the full. The enormous interest there is in flower arranging

classes and flower clubs proves that many women are sensitive to beauty and increasingly aware of their own creative powers.

Creativity, like all good gifts, is God-given. He means us to use it for our own pleasure and satisfaction. He also intends us to contribute something to the world in which we live – the world he made and continues to uphold and care for. These two things are inter-related, of course. Many of us find that we get even more pleasure out of doing things for others than out of creating something beautiful simply for our own satisfaction. This is the way God made us, and the way he always intended us to live.

Expressing feelings

It is often difficult to find the right words to tell someone that we love them. A rebellious teenager might scoff or be embarrassed if we put our feelings into words. It is not always easy to say what we would like to an undemonstrative husband, or a good friend. But we can express these things in our actions. An arrangement of tiny flowers given to a particular person, a large pedestal display to cheer a hospital waiting-room, or a posy for a new neighbour, are all ways of showing not just our love, but God's love too.

I have already mentioned my own particular physical handicap, and I don't want to dwell on it. We are all handicapped in some way – physically, emotionally, or both. Some handicaps are more obvious than others, but no one goes through life completely unscarred. It is a great thing to be able to take a hard look at ourselves and admit our limitations – and even greater to realize that no inadequacy of ours is too great for God to deal with, or too trivial for him to care about. He deals with each of us in a very individual way, as individual as the personalities he has given us. It was a great day when he came to deal with me, and I realized his love and concern for my life. Since then he has taught me how to live with my own physical handicaps. He has shown me that love is more than mere words. It is a matter of caring and sharing.

New outlook

It is amazing how this changes our whole outlook on life, and way of living. Not so long ago, I arranged flowers purely for my own pleasure. Now my greatest delight is in sharing the joy of flower arranging with others – and in the process sharing my Christian joy, of which it is just a small part. It is easy for someone with a physical handicap to make a fetish of independence, and I am no exception.

Just one of the ways in which the gift of flowers can be used. At a lunch for pensioners at my church, the flowers have been arranged by a member.

Relaxing with my husband at home, with Katie the dog.

But I can honestly say that I have no wish to return to the independence of a life in which Jesus Christ has no place. I am happy to be dependent on him.

I am just an ordinary wife and mother, and it amazes me that in the humble round of everyday life God's love can surround me all the time. To take just one example – while I have been writing this book he has taken care of so many details that the physical problems which could have arisen have been quickly solved. God's love is so very practical! And it is available to everyone who asks.

I hope this book will have encouraged you to take up flower arranging, and that your new-found hobby will bring immense satisfaction – both to you and to others. Put discouragement and frustration behind you. Relax and allow yourself to smile in appreciation of the beauty you are handling, and in anticipation of the beauty you are about to create. The past few months have been the richest and fullest yet for me. I hope the same experience will be yours too.

Index to botanical names

Garden and wild flowers have a multitude of common names which vary in different parts of the country. The list below gives the official botanical names of flowers referred to in the text, excluding those whose common names are the same as their botanical ones.

ACER, A. palmatum
ANEMONE, A. de Caen
AZALEA, A. amoenum (Rhododendron obtuson amoenum)

BERBERIS, B. irwinii
BERGENIA, B. cordifolia
BROOM, Cytisus

CAMELLIA, C. japonica
CAMPANULA, C. persicifolia
CARNATION, Dianthus caryophyllus
CATKIN, Corylus avellana
CHINESE LANTERN, Physalis
CINERARIA, C. maritima
CORNUS, C. alba spaethii
CORYDALIS, C. lutea
COTONEASTER, C. dielsiana
COW PARSLEY, Anthriscus sylvestris
COWSLIP, Veris (Cunnington's strain)
CRAB-APPLE, Malus sylvestris
CUPRESSUS, C. macrocarpa

EUPHORBIA, E. robinii

FORGET-ME-NOT, Myosotis alpestris
FOXGLOVE, Digitalis purpurea
FRENCH MARIGOLD, Tagetes patula
FUSCHIA, F. magellanica

GARDENER'S GARTERS, Phalaris arundinacea picta

GOLDEN ROD, Solidago

HARESTAILS, Lagurus
HARTS-TONGUE FERN, Scolopendrium vulgare
HEATH, Erica
HEBE, H. 'Marjorie'
HONESTY, Lunaria

KERRIA, K. japonica flore plena
KNAPWEED, Centaurea nemoralis

LARKSPUR, Delphinium ajacis hybridum
LAVENDER, Lavendula
LEOPARD'S BANE, Doronicum
LILAC, Syringa
LILY-OF-THE-VALLEY, Convallaria
LUNGWORT, Pulmonaria officinalis

MADONNA LILY, L. candidum
MAGNOLIA, M. soulangiana lennei
MARIGOLD, Calendula
MOCK ORANGE, Philadelphus 'Enchantment'
MY LADY'S BEDSTRAW, Galium verum

NASTURTIUM, Tropaeolum

ORNAMENTAL GOURD, Cucurbita

PANSY, Viola
PERIWINKLE, Vinca major variegata
POLYANTHUS, Primula vulgaris elatior
PRIVET, Ligustrum aureum
PRUNUS, P. cerasifera nigra

RAGWORT, Senecio jacobaea
ROSEBAY WILLOWHERB, Epilobium angustifolium
SANTOLINA, S. neapolitana

SCABIOUS, S. columbaria and S. atropurpurea
SILVER BIRCH, Betula pendula
SNAPDRAGON, Antirrhinum
SNOWDROP, Galanthus
SNOW-IN-SUMMER, Cerastium
SORRELL, Rumex acetosa
SPIRAEA, S. japonica
STAR-OF-THE-VELDT, Dimorphotheca
STATICE, Limonium suworowii ('Pink Poker')

STOCK, Matthiola
SWEET WILLIAM, Dianthus barbatus

THRIFT, Armeria

VARIEGATED IVY, Hedera colchica variegata

WALLFLOWER, Cheiranthus
WHITE CAMPION, Silene alba

YARROW, Achillea clypeolata